1000 Ninja Foodi Complete Cookbook 2021

Your Complete Guide to Pressure Cook, Slow Cook, Air Fry, Dehydrate, and More

1000 Ninja Foodi Recipes to Live Live

Table of Contents

What's the Ninja Foodi?

Ninja Foodi VS. Instant Pot/Slow Cooker/Air Fryer

Uncover Secret of the Revolutionary Tendercrisp Technology

Different Function Buttons of the Ninja Foodi

The Different Parts and Accessories of the Ninja Foodi

Advantages of the Ninja Foodi

Other Important Things to Remember

Useful Tips for Ninja Foodi Cooking

Frequently Asked Questions

Breakfast

    Cheesed Up Air Sticks

    Perfect Breakfast Sausage

    Excellent Mushroom And Garlic Flavored Packs

    Crispy Caramelized Morning Pop Corns

    Classic Dutch Pancakes

    Cinnamon And Pineapple Grill

    Classy Pickle Fries

    Awesome French Toasted Sticks

    Perfect Egg Pepper Cups

    Early Morning Pumpkin Muffins

    Awesome Crispy Egg Rolls

Vegetarian Mains

    Vegetable Tart

    Broccoli casserole

    Sweet sriracha carrots

    Roasted veggie mix

    Cauliflower puree with scallions

    Black beans in tomato sauce

Fish & Seafood Mains	31
Gentle And Simple Fish Stew	32
Small-Time Herby Cods	33
Hearty Swordfish Meal	34
Cool Shrimp Zoodles	35
Awesome Cherry Tomato Mackerel	36
Heartfelt Sesame Fish	37
Buttered Up Scallops	38
Poultry Mains	39
Grilled Chicken with Veggies	40
Peanut Chicken	41
Honey & Rosemary Chicken	42
Honey Chicken Wings	43
Majestic Alfredo Chicken	44
Excellent Chicken Tomatino	45
Chicken Parmesan	46
Chicken Nuggets	47
Desserts	48
Simple fruit cake	49
Egg custard	50
Peach upside-down cake	51
Chocolate pot de crème	52
Victoria sponge cake	54
Sticky toffee pudding	56
Gingerbread pudding cake	58
Appendix 1: Measurement Conversion Table Volume Equivalents (Liquid)	60
Appendix II: Healthy Food List For Weight Loss And Keto	64
8-Day Meal Plan to Enjoy Your Foodi Day By Day	71
Week 1	72

Week 2
Week 3
Week 4
Conclusion

What's the Ninja Foodi?

The Ninja Foodi is an innovative multi-hasher that comes with different features including vacuum sealing, steaming, cooking and blending. This amazing kitchen tool enables you to make delicious food hassle free. It comes with a set of two containers in which you can prepare separate **Ingredients** at the same time. With Ninja Foodi's special Double Wave discs which can chop up meat, vegetables or whatever food item you place in it into smaller pieces while keeping them intact.

Ninja Foodi VS. Instant Pot/Slow Cooker/Air Fryer

Ninja Foodi VS. Instant Pot: Instant Pot is a pressure cooker whose main features include rice cooking, slow cooking, warming, sautéing and steaming. It's not an all in one machine but it still has a number of uses. Ninja Foodi can steam, cook and blend food together unlike Instant Pot which simply cooks only rice and meat items separately. You can prepare excellent dishes in Ninja Foodi that taste like pure heaven. In fact, Ninja Foodi has a steamer that enables you to steam food that gives out a delicious aroma.

Ninja Foodi VS. Slow Cooker: Slow cookers are electric kitchen appliances used to prepare both hot and cold meals for the entire family. It's not an all in one device like Ninja Foodi but it still does many other amazing things such as slow cooking which is faster than other cooking methods, warming and sautéing food items. Slow cookers are ideal for preparing delicious meals for your family. Even though it can prepare hot meals like pasta, chicken or beef, slow cookers are not suitable for steaming and blending.

Ninja Foodi VS. Air Fryer: Both Ninja Foodi and air fryers can make delicious snacks, main dishes and desserts but there are some differences in the way these two cooking appliances work. Air fryers cook food using hot air. Air fryers don't have a steamer to steam food, their main feature is air frying which makes the food crispy like fried foods without the fat and calories.

Like air fryers, Ninja Foodi can make perfect crispy snacks and delicious main dishes but Ninja Foodi also has a steamer which can steam vegetables without adding oil. You can make healthy meals in Ninja Foodi that include steaming vegetables such as broccoli, spinach or beets for five minutes or less.

The core difference between all three of the above-mentioned appliances and the Ninja Foodi is that the Ninja Foodi is the combination of all three. Meaning, with this revolutionary kitchen appliance, you can have your cake and eat it too. The Ninja Foodi is a pressure cooker, slow cooker and an air fryer all in one. It has a Steam Cooker which enables you to steam as well as blend and cook food without adding any oil but it does this faster than slow cookers or air fryers.

Uncover Secret of the Revolutionary Tendercrisp Technology

As seen above the Ninja Foodi is an innovative multi-hasher that helps you prepare delicious food hassle free. The machine has two containers in which you can prepare separate **Ingredients** separately. With the Double Wave discs food items are chopped into smaller pieces while remaining intact.

The container is placed on the spinning arm which turn around at very high speeds making all the **Ingredients** inside it chop up finely with precision.

The Ninja Foodi is equipped with Tendercrisp technology which ensures that the Ninja Foodi can cook your food just the way you like it.

Ninja Foodi's Tendercrisp technology comes with 6 pre-set cooking methods which are:

1. **Steaming:** This method is used to prepare steamed food. This steaming system is unique and quite different from the traditional steamers that are used in Asian kitchens. Traditional steamers are able to steam only one item at a time. Whereas, this steamer is able to steam five different items at a time. This steamer cooks food in less than two minutes so you can have your food cooked quickly without any hassle. Also, this method is not messy as it eliminates the wastage of water or juices from various food items like meat and vegetables which splash around during cooking. Ninja Foodi steam vegetables like broccoli, spinach or beets in less than two minutes. These vegetables are healthier as they retain all the nutrients in them and provide you with a lot of vitamins and fiber. Ninja Foodi's steamer is equipped with steam control which enables you to adjust the steam output as per your requirements. There are three different levels of steam output that can be adjusted namely low, high and off. This lets you decide how much steam will be released during cooking according to your preference so that it can remain healthy as well as delicious.
2. **Boiling:** This is used to prepare boiled food items such as rice, pasta, chicken or vegetables.
3. **Browning:** This mode is used to prepare crispy snacks like potato chips or French fries. It does this by cooking the food item using both air and convection heat at the same time.
4. **Sauté:** This is another unique feature as it is not found in any other kitchen appliance available in the market right now. This feature is used to prepare food items like stew, paella or risotto. Here, the speed of the blades is adjusted according to the requirement as it cooks your food item in a mix of air and convection heat.
5. **Fry:** This is used to prepare crispy snacks like French fries or potato chips byusing both pressure and convection heat simultaneously.
6. **Bake:** This mode is used to prepare sweet and savory dishes like cakes, brownies, or lasagna. It contains a baking pan that has been given a non-stick coating so that your food doesn't stick to the inner sides of the pan. The Ninja Foodi also equipped with a cooking timer which has three different modes namely 30 minutes, 1 hour and 2 hours.

Ninja Foodi's interchangeable containers ensure that you have separate compartments for both baking and cooking food items separately.

Different Function Buttons of the Ninja Foodi

I have tried to outline the basic functions of all of the buttons present in most models of the Ninja Foodi.

Pressure: This button will be present only in the models that have pressure feature. This is used to cook food by generating high pressure inside the cooking pot.

Steam: This button is present only in models of Foodi which have a steaming function. It is used to cook food by generating steam of high temperature inside the cooking pot.

Spin: This button is not present in all models but it can be found mostly in models that have interchangeable containers like bowl pitcher and steamer etc. This button is used to rotate the containers with food items inside them.

Cooking Timer: This is present in most of the models of Ninja Foodi which helps you to time you're cooking so that it doesn't get overcooked. You can set the timer from anywhere between

Slow Cooker: This mode is present in most of the Foodi model. It is called slow cooker mode because it is used to cook food in low, steady temperature for longer period of time. The slow cooker mode is very useful if you wish to prepare soups or stews or chili as you can leave the food item in the pot and let it cook on low heat and still be sure that it doesn't burn or overcook.

Start/Stop Button: This is present in all models of Ninja Foodi. It is used to start or stop the cooking process.

Sabbath Mode: This mode is found in huge number of Ninja Foodi models like model FBA and some models of Pro series like PF770. This mode is used to prepare food on low heat which means you can prepare your food for Sabbath or any other religious festivals.

Sear/Saute: This mode is mostly found in models with interchangeable containers. You place the food item in this container and set the temperature to high so that you are able to brown or sear the food.

Air Crisp: This mode is present in several models like FBA and Pro series like PF770 as well. This mode ensures that your food does not get soggy.

Air Fry: This mode is present in some models like FBA and Pro series like PFS770, PF770 etc. It is used to fry food items without using any oil or butter.

The nutrition facts are calculated based on a recipe of 1390 calories on high heat and cooking time of 40 minutes.

Bake/Roast: If you use bake/roast instead of fry. The nutrition facts are calculated based on a recipe of 700 calories on medium heat and cooking time of one hour

Confit: Instead of shallow frying, if you roast the food item in the oil, then it is called confit. The nutrition facts are calculated based on a recipe of 1300 calories on high heat and cooking time of 2 hours 3 minutes.

Broil: The broiler is an extra feature that is available in several models of Ninja Foodi. It is a type of cooking method used in ovens which uses direct heat to cook food. The broiler can be used to cook food items like salmon, chicken or steak.

Dehydrate: This mode is used to dehydrate food in the Ninja Foodi by heating up the air inside it. This helps to preserve and store your food items so that they can't become rotten, rancid, or discolored for a longer period of time.

The Different Parts and Accessories of the Ninja Foodi

The different parts of the Ninja Foodi are as follows:

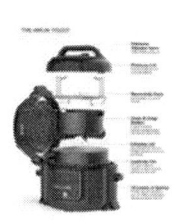

- ❖ **Pressure Release Valve:** This is an important component of the Ninja Foodi. It is used to release the pressure built up in the pot. The Pressure Release Valve should be opened during pressure cooking and should also be opened at regular intervals during cooking as well. This ensures that excess steam and air can escape from inside the Cooking Pot so that it doesn't cause any damage to your Ninja Foodi.
- ❖ **Pressure Lid:** This is another important component of the cooking pot. You should not touch or open the Lid while it is in pressure cooking mode. The lid is able to withstand high pressures and can cause burns if handled improperly.
- ❖ **Crisping Lid:** This is the lid that is used to cook your food in Air Crisp mode. It is recommended to follow the recipe instructions carefully while preparing food in air crisping mode.
- ❖ **Cooking Pot:** This is a part of the device that enables you to prepare various recipes on different modes. The cooking pot has two containers on top of each other so that you can serve or store your food separately.

Asides from the above-mentioned core parts, there are some others that you should know about as well

The Reversible Rack: This is used to cook food manually and it is present in most models of the Ninja Foodi. If the rack doesn't come with a model, you can buy it separately as an accessory.

Cook And Crisp Basket: This is another useful accessory that is used to cook food in air fry mode.

Extra Reversible Rack/ 8 Inch Round Wire Cooling Rack: This is used to cool your food items easily.

Extra Sealing Ring: This is used to seal the Foodi perfectly.

The 10 Piece Multipurpose Cooking Discs: These discs are used to chop different food items finely and evenly.

Multi-Purpose Pan/Metal/Ceramic Bowl: These are used to cook your food in steaming, sautéing or boiling mode.

Roasting Rack Insert: This is used to cook your food in the oven.

Cook and Crisp Layered Insert: This is a 9 inch round tray which can be used on Air Fry mode.

Advantages of the Ninja Foodi

The Ninja Foodi has many advantages which make it stand out from other kitchen appliances available in the market. Here are some of its most prominent advantages:

- **Simplicity:** The Ninja Foodi is extremely easy to use. The recipes that you use can be cooked in various cooking modes and still taste great no matter what you cook. The Ninja Foodi is simple to operate as well as it does not require any skills to be able to prepare food in less than 15 minutes using this device. You can prepare healthy and tasty food in a matter of minutes. This device is extremely easy to use, clean and maintain which makes it the most preferred kitchen appliance of today's time. The recipe book that comes with the Ninja Foodi is very useful as it has many recipes for you to choose from. Ninja Foodi comes with a manual that explains everything about how to operate the device and use its features easily. The mode selection panel is also very simple to understand so that you can cook delicious food items easily.

- **Flexibility:** Another thing that makes it stand out from other kitchen appliances is its flexibility. You can use the Ninja Foodi to prepare various recipes like soups, stews, chili in slow cooker mode. You can also use the Ninja Foodi to prepare anything from meat to vegetables and from curries to cakes and cookies. The different modes of the Ninja Foodi make sure that you are able to prepare everything on a single device without having to purchase any other item for cooking your favorite food items.

- **Versatility:** You can prepare food items like cakes, cookies, roasts, French fries, and other snack items by using the Ninja Foodi. This makes it very useful for a large number of people. You can use this device to prepare your favorite dessert for the family or you can also use it to prepare food for parties or special occasions.

- **Safety:** Using the Ninja Foodi is extremely safe as you do not have to handle any hot cooking pot directly. You can prepare your food without having to handle the hot cooking pot directly as you can place the cooking pot inside the oven and prepare your favorite food items in it.

- **Efficiency:** This is the most important advantage of this device. You will be able to save a large amount of money by using this device. This appliance helps you to prepare your favorite food items in a faster and much more efficient way as compared to other kitchen appliances available now. You will be able to save much more time by using this device as it only requires less than 15 minutes to prepare food. This device also saves your energy and fuel which means you can save a lot of electricity. You can also reduce your monthly supply bills by using this device due to the fact that it is extremely energy efficient.

- **Portability:** The Ninja Foodi is extremely portable as you can use it at home or take it anywhere with you in your car or even on camping trips. It is extremely lightweight so that you can carry it around easily. This device also has a small storage size so that you can place it anywhere in your kitchen without having to worry about whether there is enough space to place the device or not.

- **Variety:** Ninja Foodi allows you to choose from many different types of recipes like cakes, cookies, roasts, French fries, soup and stews and much more. You can prepare anything on the Ninja Foodi without worrying about results as it will always turn out perfectly.

Other Important Things to Remember

If you have never used this device before, it is recommended for you to read the instructions carefully so that you can operate the device efficiently and use its features without any problem. It is also recommended for you to follow the instructions carefully when using this device. The Ninja Foodi comes with a recipe book which is very useful as it will help you prepare different food items easily. The recipe book not only contains recipes but it also has instructions on how to use the features of this device.

Useful Tips for Ninja Foodi Cooking

As time goes on, you will learn how to utilize the power of your Ninja Foodi to its full extent.

However, the following tips will help you during the early days of your life with the Foodi and ensure that your experience is as pleasant and smooth as possible.

- It is crucial that you don't just press the function buttons randomly! Reading through the recipe book will give you a good idea of how to use each function.
- One of the basic functions is to be able to press the start/stop button when you are planning to cook a particular recipe. This way, you'll be able to get an idea about how much time it takes for your dishes to be prepared.
- You should also check out the cooking chart that comes with all Foodi models. This chart will tell you how long each menu item takes to be prepared. You can also figure out which mode is best suited for your **Ingredients**.
- Using the sealing ring that comes with your Foodi model is quite easy as it seals the appliance perfectly and protects from any sort of damage.

It is recommended for people who aren't aware of how to use this device to take help from more experienced people during their initial few times using this appliance. You should also try to read the instructions given by Ninja Foodi as it will help you to operate the device and use its features efficiently.

Frequently Asked Questions

This section will answer all your burning questions related to the Ninja Foodi product.

Why do some foods such as French fries, not get fried well in the Foodi?

The reason for this is that most of the food items that are fried usually have a high water content. This type of food requires a longer cooking time as compared to other food items. However, you can learn more about this by reading through the recipe book that comes with the device. The recipe book has all the information about how to prepare various recipes using this device.

Is it possible to prepare baking dough using the Foodi?

Yes, you can prepare baking dough with a little bit of creativity using the Foodi. What you will need to do is to prepare your baking dough on any other device before placing it on the Foodi. However, if you prefer a more convenient option for this, you can simply place the dough from inside its packaging and set it to cook on Bake mode. You will find that the cooking time for this particular recipe is much shorter than making your own dough.

How do you use the Ninja Foodi for preparing steamed food?

You will have to use a steamer basket when you are planning to prepare any type of steamed food using this device.

If you aren't aware of how to use the basket, here is a useful tip: All you need to do is to place the steamer basket inside the Cooking Pot and pour water until it reaches the level specified in each recipe. You will then have to press start and wait for your food to be prepared.

The device is not heating properly. What can be the possible reasons for this?

The main reason why this might happen is due to overheating. You can remedy overheating quickly by turning the device off and then place it in a vented area for a while. You should also avoid using any type of sharp or hard objects around the Cooking Pot as you could end up damaging your device in case of any accident.

The Foodi is not working properly. What can be the possible reasons for this?

The main reason for your Foodi not working properly is the fact that you have not read through the instructions before using your device. This is an extremely important step and you should follow it every time you use your device. You should also avoid adding too much food in the Cooking Pot at a single time so that this doesn't affect the functioning of the device.

Breakfast

Cheesed Up Air Sticks

Ingredients:

- 6 cheese sticks, snake-sized
- 60 ml parmesan cheese, grated
- 2 eggs
- 15 ml Italian seasoning
- 60 ml flour, whole wheat
- 3.75 ml rosemary, grounded
- 15 ml garlic powder

Directions:

1. Take cheese sticks and set aside
2. Take a shallow bowl and beat eggs into the bowl
3. Mix cheese, flour, and seasonings in another bowl
4. Roll the cheese sticks in the eggs and then in the batter
5. Now do the process again till the sticks as well coated
6. Set temperature of zone 1 to 190 degrees C and time to 7 minutes
7. Select MATCH COOK to copy settings of zone 1 to zone 2
8. Divide the cheese sticks into Baskets and cook
9. Serve and enjoy!

Nutritional Contents:
Calories: 50 Fat: 2g Carbohydrates: 3g Protein: 2g

Perfect Breakfast Sausage

Ingredients:

- ~ 1 pinch sriracha flakes
- ~ 1 pinch salt and pepper
- ~ 5 ml olive oil
- ~ 8 whole eggs
- ~ 2 bell pepper, halved, seeds removed

Directions:

1. Divide the sausages in the two Air fryer baskets.
2. Return the Air Fryer Baskets to the Air Fryer.
3. Select the Air Fryer mode for Zone 1 with 198 degrees C temperature and 13 minutes cooking time.
4. Press the MATCH COOK button to copy the settings for Zone 2.
5. Initiate cooking by pressing the START/PAUSE BUTTON.
6. Serve warm and fresh.

Nutritional Contents:
Calories: 187 Carbohydrate: 8g Protein: 24g Fat: 6g

Excellent Mushroom And Garlic Flavored Packs

Ingredients:

- ~ 16 small button mushrooms
- ~ 1 and 1/2 slice white bread
- ~ 1 garlic clove, crushed
- ~ 15 ml flat-leaf parsley, chopped
- ~ Black pepper to taste
- ~ 22.5 ml olive oil

Directions:

1. Set temperature of Zone 1 of Air Fryer to 198 degrees C, set time to 9 minutes
2. Use MATCH COOK to copy settings from Zone 1 to Zone 2
3. Take a food processor and add bread slices, garlic, pepper, and parsley
4. Grind them up until a crumb-like texture is achieved
5. Add olive oil to the crumb mix and stir well
6. Take your mushrooms and prepare them by cutting off the stalks
7. Fill the cap with the crumb mixture
8. Pat any excess crumbs off
9. Divide the mushrooms between both zones, and let them cook until golden brown
10. Serve and enjoy once done!

Nutritional Contents:
Calories: 240 Carbohydrate: 28g Protein: 3g Fat: 14g

Crispy Caramelized Morning Pop Corns

Ingredients:

- 2 Litre popcorn
- 250 ml butter
- 250 ml of sugar
- 75 ml whipped cream

Directions:

1. Set temperature of Zone 1 to 115 degrees C and set timer to 5 minutes
2. Click MATCH COOK to copy settings from zone 1 to zone 2
3. Divide the corns between the two zones and cook for 5 minutes
4. Transfer them to a bowl
5. Take a large bowl and put the popcorn in the bowl
6. Mix butter, sugar, and cream and heat over medium heat stirring constantly. The sauce should be boiling; continue boiling until the mixture reaches the softball stage 115 C.
7. Remove mixture from heat and pour over popcorn, stirring until all popcorn is well coated. Be sure to serve it right away.
8. Enjoy!

Nutritional Contents:
Calories: 120 Fat: 2.5g Carbohydrates: 25g Protein: 1g

Classic Dutch Pancakes

Ingredients:

- ~ 3 eggs
- ~ 30 ml unsalted butter
- ~ 125 ml flour
- ~ 30 ml sugar, powdered
- ~ 125 ml milk
- ~ 375 ml fresh strawberries, sliced

Directions:

1. Set temperature of Zone 1 to 165 degrees C and set bake mode, set timer to 15 minutes
2. Click MATCH COOK to copy settings from zone 1 to zone 2
3. Heat with a 6-by-6-by-2 inch pan in the Basket and add the butter and heat until the butter melts.
4. Take a medium-sized bowl and add flour, milk, eggs, and vanilla.
5. Beat them well with an eggbeater until combined and frothy.
6. Divide the batter between the two baskets, or place the direction of the pan inside if possible
7. Bake for 12 to 16 minutes or until the pancake is puffed and golden brown.
8. Remove from the oven and drizzle them with powdered sugar and strawberries.
9. Serve immediately and enjoy!

Nutritional Contents:
Calories: 196 Fat: 9g Carbohydrates: 19g Protein: 16g

Cinnamon And Pineapple Grill

Ingredients:

- 5 ml cinnamon
- 5 pineapple slices
- 125 ml brown sugar

Directions:

1. Make a mix of cinnamon with brown sugar.
2. Cover the pineapple slices with the mixture.
3. Let the pineapple slices rest for 20 minutes.
4. Divide the pineapple slices between the two zones
5. Set the temperature of zone 1 to 170 degrees C and cook time to 10 minutes
6. Press MATCH COOK to copy settings from zone 1 to zone 2
7. Let it cook for 10 minutes, flip the pineapple slices and cook for 10 minutes more
8. Serve with basil and honey!

Nutritional Contents:
Calories: 480 Fat: 18g Carbohydrates: 71g Protein: 13g

Classy Pickle Fries

Ingredients:

- ~ 24 hamburger dill pickle chips
- ~ 75 ml whole-wheat panko breadcrumbs
- ~ 1.25 ml garlic powder
- ~ 60 ml (2 large) egg white or fat-free liquid egg
- ~ Dash cayenne pepper
- ~ 1.25 ml onion powder
- ~ Ketchup. to dip
- ~ Dash each salt and black pepper

Directions:

1. Grease the baskets of both zones with a bit of oil
2. Set temperature of Zone 1 to 85 degrees C and set BAKE mode, set timer to 20 minutes
3. Select MATCH COOK to copy settings of zone 1 to zone 2
4. Take a bowl and mix breadcrumbs with seasoning into it
5. Blot pickle chips dry
6. Transfer them into a medium-small bowl
7. Coat with egg whites to both sides
8. Remove the excess eggs and then coat with seasoned
9. Bake for 10 minutes
10. Bake 10 minutes more to make it crispy
11. Serve and enjoy!

Nutritional Contents:
Calories: 59 Fat: 0.5g Carbohydrates: 11.5g Protein: 2.5g

Awesome French Toasted Sticks

Ingredients:

- ~ 5 ml icing sugar
- ~ 1 pinch ground clove
- ~ 1 pinch nutmeg ground
- ~ 1 pinch cinnamon, ground
- ~ 1 pinch salt
- ~ 2 eggs, beaten
- ~ 30 ml butter
- ~ 4 pieces of bread

Directions:

1. Add two eggs to a mixing bowl and stir cinnamon, nutmeg, ground cloves, and salt, then whisk well.
2. Spread butter on both sides of the bread slices and cut them into thick strips.
3. Dip the breadsticks in the egg mixture and place them in the two Air Fryer baskets.
4. Return the Air Fryer Baskets to the Air Fryer.
5. Select the Air Fryer mode for Zone 1 with 198 degrees C temperature and 8 minutes cooking time.
6. Press the MATCH COOK button to copy the settings for Zone 2.
7. Initiate cooking by pressing the START/PAUSE BUTTON.
8. Flip the French toast sticks when cooked halfway through.
9. Serve.

Nutritional Contents:
Calories: 391 Carbohydrate: 36g Protein: 6g Fat: 3g

Perfect Egg Pepper Cups

Ingredients:

- 1 pinch sriracha flakes
- 1 pinch salt and pepper
- 5 ml olive oil
- 8 whole eggs
- 2 bell pepper, halved and seeds removed

Directions:

1. Slice the bell peppers in half, lengthwise, and remove their seeds and the inner portion to get a cup-like shape.
2. Rub olive oil on the edges of the bell peppers.
3. Place them in the two Air Fryer Baskets with their cut side up and crack two eggs in each half of bell pepper.
4. Drizzle salt, black pepper, and sriracha flakes on top of the eggs.
5. Return the Air Fryer Baskets to the Air Fryer.
6. Select the Air Fryer mode for Zone 1 with 198 degrees C temperature and 18 minutes cooking time.
7. Press the MATCH COOK button to copy the settings for Zone 2.
8. Initiate cooking by pressing the START/PAUSE BUTTON.
9. Serve warm and fresh.

Nutritional Contents:
Calories: 212 Carbohydrate: 14g Protein: 20g Fat: 11g

Early Morning Pumpkin Muffins

Ingredients:

- ~ 2.5 ml nutmeg
- ~ Cooking spray
- ~ 7.5 ml vanilla essence
- ~ 7.5 ml cocoa nib
- ~ 2.5 ml coconut butter
- ~ 1 medium egg, beaten
- ~ 60 ml honey
- ~ 250 ml gluten-free oats
- ~ 125 ml pumpkin free oats

Directions:

1. Add oats, honey, eggs, pumpkin puree, coconut butter, cocoa nibs, vanilla essence, and nutmeg to a bowl and mix well until smooth.
2. Divide the batter into two 4-cups muffin trays, greased with cooking spray.
3. Place one mini muffin tray in each of the two Air Fryer Baskets.
4. Return the Air Fryer Baskets to the Air Fryer.
5. Select the Air Fryer mode for Zone 1 with 85 degrees C temperature and 13 minutes cooking time.
6. Press the MATCH COOK button to copy the settings for Zone 2.
7. Initiate cooking by pressing the START/PAUSE BUTTON.
8. Allow the muffins to cool, then serve.

Nutritional Contents:
Calories: 138 Carbohydrate: 32g Protein: 10g Fat: 10g

Awesome Crispy Egg Rolls

Ingredients:

- 250 ml of water
- 15 ml olive oil
- 6 egg roll wrappers
- 2 sausage patties
- 125 ml cheddar cheese, shredded
- Salt and pepper to taste
- 15 ml milk
- 2 whole eggs

Directions:

1. Grease the same skillet with 5 ml olive oil and pour the egg mixture into it.
2. Stir cook to make scrambled eggs.
3. Add sausage, mix well and remove the skillet from the heat.
4. Spread an egg roll wrapper on the working surface in a diamond shape position.
5. Add 15ml of cheese at the bottom third of the roll wrapper.
6. Top the cheese with egg mixture and wet the edges of the wrapper with water.
7. Fold the two corners of the wrapper and roll it, then seal the edges.
8. Repeat the same steps and divide the rolls in the two Air Fryer Baskets.
9. Return the Air Fryer Baskets to the Air Fryer.
10. Select the Air Fryer mode for Zone 1 with 85 degrees C temperature and 13 minutes cooking time.
11. Press the MATCH COOK button to copy the settings for Zone 2.
12. Initiate cooking by pressing the START/PAUSE BUTTON.
13. Flip the rolls after 8 minutes and continue cooking for another 5 minutes.
14. Serve warm and fresh.

Nutritional Contents:
Calories: 322 Carbohydrate: 14g Protein: 17g Fat: 111g

Vegetarian Mains

Vegetable Tart

Ingredients

- 200g puff pastry
- 1 egg yolk
- 2 red bell peppers
- 140g tomatoes
- 1 red onion
- 1 eggplant
- 85g zucchini
- 5 ml salt
- 5 ml olive oil
- 5 ml ground black pepper
- 15 ml turmeric
- 200g goat cheese
- 60 ml cream

Directions:

1. Whisk the egg yolk, combine it with the ground black pepper and stir well.
2. Roll the puff pastry using a rolling pin. Spray the pressure cooker with the olive oil inside and add the puff pastry.
3. Spread the puff pastry with the whisked egg. Chop the tomatoes and dice the onions. Chop the eggplants and zucchini.
4. Combine the vegetables together and sprinkle them with the salt, turmeric, and cream. Mix well and place the vegetable mixture in the pressure cooker.
5. Chop the red bell peppers and sprinkle the pressure cooker mixture with them. Grate the goat cheese and sprinkle the tart with the cheese.
6. Close the pressure cooker lid Cook at Pressure mode for 25 minutes. When the dish is cooked, release the pressure and open the pressure cooker lid. Check if the tart is cooked and remove it from the pressure cooker.
7. Cut the tart into slices and serve it.

Nutritional Value Per Serving:
Calories 279, Fats 18.8 g, Carbohydrates 18.42 g, Protein 10 g

Broccoli casserole

Ingredients

- 280g broccoli
- 250 ml cream
- 200g mushrooms
- 1 onion
- 1 bell pepper
- 125 ml chicken stock
- 225g crackers
- 15 ml butter
- 5 ml ground black pepper
- 15 ml salt
- 75 ml green peas

Directions:

1. Chop the broccoli and slice the mushrooms. Crush the crackers and combine them with the ground black pepper and stir well.
2. Chop the bell pepper and onion. Place the broccoli in the pressure cooker. Make a layer with the bell pepper and onion.
3. Combine the cream and salt together. Stir the mixture and add the green peas.
4. Pour the cream mixture in the pressure cooker. Add chicken stock and butter. Sprinkle the casserole mixture with the crushed crackers.
5. Close the pressure cooker lid and cook the dish on Sauté mode for 25 minutes.
6. When the cooking time ends, let the dish rest briefly before serving.

Nutritional Value Per Serving:
Calories 317, Fats 15.4 g, Carbohydrates 41.89 g, Protein 7 g

Sweet sriracha carrots

Ingredients

- 30 ml sriracha
- 250 ml of water
- 5 ml Erythritol
- 30 ml olive oil
- 125 ml dill
- 450g carrots
- 5 ml oregano

Directions:

1. Wash the carrots, peel them, and slice them. Set the pressure cooker to Sauté mode. Pour the olive oil into the pressure cooker and add the sliced carrots.
2. Sprinkle the vegetables with the oregano and dill. Sauté the dish for 15 minutes, stirring frequently.
3. Sprinkle the carrot with Erythritol, water, and sriracha. Mix well.
4. Close the pressure cooker lid and cook the dish on Pressure mode for 2 minutes.
5. When the cooking time ends, release the remaining pressure and open the pressure cooker lid. Transfer the carrots to a serving plate.

Nutritional Value Per Serving:
Calories 74, Fat 4.2g, Carbohydrates 9.3g, Protein 1.2g

Roasted veggie mix

Ingredients

- 2 eggplants
- 2 bell peppers
- 15 ml salt
- 225g tomatoes
- 2 turnips
- 1 zucchini
- 15 ml oregano
- 2 carrots
- 45 ml sesame oil
- 1 litre beef broth

Directions:

1. Peel the eggplants and chop them. Sprinkle the eggplants with the salt and stir well. Remove the seeds from the bell peppers and chop them.
2. Slice the tomatoes and chop turnips. Chop the zucchini.
3. Peel the carrots and grate them. Transfer all the vegetables to the pressure cooker. Add the oregano, sesame oil, and beef broth.
4. Mix well and close the pressure cooker lid. Cook the dish on Steam mode for 30 minutes.
5. When the cooking time ends, transfer the dish to serving bowls.

Nutritional Value Per Serving:
Calories 107, Fats 5 g, Carbohydrates 13.2 g, Protein 4 g

Cauliflower puree with scallions

Ingredients

- ~ 1 head cauliflower
- ~ 1 litre of water
- ~ 15 ml salt
- ~ 60 ml butter
- ~ 85g scallions
- ~ 5 ml chicken stock
- ~ 1.25 ml sesame seeds
- ~ 1 egg yolk

Directions:

1. Wash the cauliflower and chop it roughly. Place the cauliflower in the pressure cooker.
2. Add the water and salt. Close the pressure cooker lid and cook the vegetableson Pressure mode for 5 minutes.
3. Release the pressure and open the pressure cooker lid. Remove the cauliflower from the pressure cooker and let it rest briefly.
4. Place the cauliflower in a blender. Add the butter, chicken stock, and sesame seeds. Blend the mixture well.
5. Chop the scallions. Add the egg yolk to the blender and blend the mixture for 30 seconds. Remove the cauliflower puree from the blender and combine it with the scallions.
6. Mix well and serve.

Nutritional Value Per Serving:
Calories 94, Fats 8.7 g, Carbohydrates 3.39 g, Protein 2 g

Black beans in tomato sauce

Ingredients

- 225g black beans
- 1 onion
- 250 ml tomato paste
- 15 ml minced garlic
- 5 ml ground black pepper
- 115g celery stalk
- 1 litre chicken stock
- 2.5 ml chile pepper
- 2.5 ml turmeric

Directions:

1. Place the black beans in the pressure cooker. Peel the onion and chop it. Add the tomato paste, garlic, ground black pepper.
2. Chicken stock chile pepper and turmeric in the pressure cooker. Mix well and close the pressure cooker lid.
3. Cook the dish on Pressure mode for 15 minutes. When the cooking time ends, release the pressure and open the pressure cooker lid.
4. Add the chopped onion and mix well. Close the pressure cooker lid and cook the dish on Sauté mode for 4 minutes
5. Open the pressure cooker lid and mix well. Transfer the cooked dish to a serving bowl.

Nutritional Value Per Serving:
Calories 109, Fats 2.1 g, Carbohydrates 17.59 g, Protein 6 g

Fish & Seafood Mains

Gentle And Simple Fish Stew

Ingredients

- 750 ml fish stock
- 1 onion, diced
- 250 ml broccoli, chopped
- 450 ml celery stalks, chopped
- 375 ml cauliflower, diced
- 1 carrot, sliced
- 450g white fish fillets, chopped
- 250 ml heavy cream
- 1 bay leaf
- 30 ml butter
- 1.25 ml pepper
- 2.5 ml salt
- 1.25 ml garlic powder

Directions

1. Set your Ninja Foodi to Saute mode and add butter, let it melt
2. Add onion and carrots, cook for 3 minutes
3. Stir in remaining **Ingredients**
4. Lock lid and cook on HIGH pressure for 4 minutes
5. Naturally, release pressure over 10 minutes
6. Discard bay leaf
7. Serve and enjoy!

Nutrition Values (Per Serving)
Calories: 298 Fat: 18g Carbohydrates: 6g Protein: 24g

Small-Time Herby Cods

Ingredients

- 4 garlic cloves, minced
- 10 ml coconut aminos
- 60 ml butter
- 6 whole eggs
- 2 small onions, chopped
- 3 (115g each) skinless cod fish fillets, cut into rectangular pieces
- 2 green chilies, chopped
- Salt and pepper to taste

Directions

1. Take a shallow dish and add all **Ingredients** except cod, beat the mixture well
2. Dip each fillet into the mixture and keep it on the side
3. Transfer prepared fillets to your Ninja Foodi Crisping basket and transfer basket to Pot
4. Lock Crisping lid and cook on "Air Crisp" mode for 8 minutes at 165 degrees C
5. Serve and enjoy!

Nutrition Values (Per Serving)
Calories: 409 Fat: 25g Carbohydrates: 7g Protein: 37g

Hearty Swordfish Meal

Ingredients

- 5 swordfish fillets
- 125 ml of melted clarified butter
- 6 garlic cloves, chopped
- 15 ml black pepper

Directions

1. Take a mixing bowl and add garlic, clarified butter, black pepper
2. Take a parchment paper and add the fillet
3. Cover and wrap the fish
4. Keep repeating until the fillets are wrapped up
5. Transfer wrapped fish to Ninja Foodi pot and lock lid
6. Allow them to cook for 2 and a ½ hour at high pressure
7. Release the pressure naturally
8. Serve and enjoy!

Nutrition Values (Per Serving)
Calories: 379 Fat: 26g Carbohydrates: 1g Protein: 34g

Cool Shrimp Zoodles

Ingredients

- 1 litre zoodles
- 15 ml basil, chopped
- 30 ml Ghee
- 250 ml vegetable stock
- 2 garlic cloves, minced
- 30 ml olive oil
- ½ lemon
- 2.5 ml paprika

Directions

1. Set your Ninja Foodi to Saute mode and add ghee, let it heat up
2. Add olive oil as well
3. Add garlic and cook for 1 minute
4. Add lemon juice, shrimp and cook for 1 minute
5. Stir in rest of the **Ingredients** and lock lid, cook on LOW pressure for 5 minutes
6. Quick release pressure and serve
7. Enjoy!

Nutrition Values (Per Serving)
Calories: 277 Fat: 6g Carbohydrates: 5g Protein: 27g

Awesome Cherry Tomato Mackerel

Ingredients

- ~ 4 Mackerel fillets
- ~ 1.25 ml onion powder
- ~ 1.25 ml lemon powder
- ~ 1.25 ml garlic powder
- ~ 2.5 ml salt
- ~ 450 ml cherry tomatoes
- ~ 45 ml melted butter
- ~ 375 ml of water
- ~ 15 ml black olives

Directions

1. Grease baking dish and arrange cherry tomatoes at the bottom of the dish
2. Top with fillets sprinkle all spices
3. Drizzle melted butter over
4. Add water to your Ninja Foodi
5. Lower rack in Ninja Foodi and place baking dish on top of the rack
6. Lock lid and cook on LOW pressure for 7 minutes
7. Quick release pressure
8. Serve and enjoy!

Nutrition Values (Per Serving)
Calories: 325 Fat: 24g Carbohydrates: 2g Protein: 21g

Heartfelt Sesame Fish

Ingredients

- 675g salmon fillet
- 5 ml sesame seeds
- 5 ml butter, melted
- 2.5 ml salt
- 15 ml apple cider vinegar
- 1.25 ml rosemary, dried

Directions

1. Take apple cider vinegar and spray it to the salmon fillets
2. Then add dried rosemary, sesame seeds, butter and salt
3. Mix them well
4. Take butter sauce and brush the salmon properly
5. Place the salmon on the rack and lower the air fryer lid
6. Set the air fryer mode
7. Cook the fish for 8 minutes at 180 C
8. Serve hot and enjoy!

Nutrition Values (Per Serving)
Calories: 239 Fat: 11.2g Carbohydrates: 0.3g Protein: 33.1g

Buttered Up Scallops

Ingredients

- ~ 4 garlic cloves, minced
- ~ 60 ml rosemary, chopped
- ~ 900g sea scallops
- ~ 3 litre butter
- ~ Salt and pepper to taste

Directions

1. Set your Ninja Foodi to Saute mode and add butter, rosemary, and garlic
2. Saute for 1 minute
3. Add scallops, salt, and pepper
4. Saute for 2 minutes
5. Lock Crisping lid and Crisp for 3 minutes at 175 degrees C
6. Serve and enjoy!

Nutrition Values (Per Serving)
Calories: 279 Fat: 16g Carbohydrates: 5g Protein: 25g

Poultry Mains

Grilled Chicken with Veggies

Ingredients:

- 2 chicken thighs and legs
- 30 ml oil, divided
- Salt and pepper to taste
- 1 onion, diced
- 60 ml mushrooms, sliced
- 250 ml potatoes, diced
- 15 ml lemon juice
- 15 ml honey
- 4 sprigs fresh thyme, chopped
- 2 cloves garlic, crushed and minced

Directions:

1. Add the grill grate to your Ninja Foodi Grill.
2. Put the veggie tray on top of the grill grate.
3. Close the hood.
4. Choose the grill function and set it to high.
5. Press Start to preheat.
6. Brush the chicken with half of the oil.
7. Season with salt and pepper.
8. Toss the onion, mushrooms, and potatoes in the remaining oil.
9. Sprinkle with salt and pepper.
10. Add chicken to the grill grate.
11. Add the potato mixture to the veggie tray.
12. Close the hood and cook for 10 to 15 minutes.
13. Flip chicken and toss potatoes.
14. Cook for another 10 minutes.
15. Serving Suggestions:
16. Serve chicken with the veggies on the side. Garnish with herb sprigs.

Nutritional Values (Per Serving)
Calories: 178 Fat: 13 g Carbohydrates: 6 g Protein: 20 g

Peanut Chicken

Ingredients:

- 675g. chicken breast, sliced into cubes
- Salt to taste
- 5 ml oil
- 3 clove garlic, chopped
- 15 ml ginger, chopped
- 365g coconut milk
- 45 ml soy sauce
- 45 ml honey
- 30 ml fresh lime juice
- 15 ml chili garlic paste
- 125 ml peanut butter

Directions:

1. Season the chicken with salt. Set the Ninja Foodi to Sauté. Add the oil.
2. Cook the garlic and ginger for 1 minute.
3. Add the chicken and all the other **Ingredients** except the peanut butter.
4. Mix well. Put the peanut butter on top of the chicken but do not stir.
5. Seal the pot. Set it to Pressure. Cook at high pressure for 9 minutes.
6. Release the pressure naturally.
7. Serving Suggestion:
8. Serve on top of spinach leaves.

Nutritional Information Per Serving:
Calories: 445 Total Fat: 29.1 g Saturated Fat: 15.4 g Cholesterol: 73 mg Sodium: 645 mg Total Carbohydrate: 18 g Dietary Fiber: 2.9 g Total Sugars: 12.9 g Protein: 31.5 g Potassium: 762 mg

Honey & Rosemary Chicken

Ingredients:

- 5 ml paprika
- Salt to taste
- 2.5 ml baking powder
- 900g chicken wings
- 60 ml honey
- 15 ml lemon juice
- 15 ml garlic, minced
- 15 ml rosemary, chopped

Directions:

1. Choose the Air Fry setting on your Ninja Foodi Grill.
2. Set it to 198°C.
3. Set the time to 30 minutes.
4. Press Start to preheat.
5. While waiting, mix the paprika, salt, and baking powder in a bowl.
6. Add the wings to the crisper basket.
7. Close and cook for 15 minutes.
8. Flip and cook for another 15 minutes.
9. In a bowl, mix the remaining **Ingredients**.
10. Coat the wings with the sauce and cook for another 5 minutes.
11. Serving Suggestions:
12. Serve with the remaining sauce.

Nutritional Values (Per Serving)
Calories: 438 Fat: 36 g Carbohydrates: 8 g Protein: 22 g

Honey Chicken Wings

Ingredients:

- 450g chicken wings
- 60 ml honey
- 30 ml hot sauce
- 22.5 ml soy sauce
- 15 ml butter
- 15 ml lime juice

Directions:

1. Place the chicken wings in the Ninja Foodi basket. Add the basket to the pot.
2. Cover the crisping lid. Set it to Air Crisp. Cook at 180°C for 30 minutes.
3. Flip every 10 minutes. Remove the wings and set aside. Set the pot to Sauté.
4. Add the rest of the Ingredients and mix well. Simmer for 3 minutes.
5. Toss the wings in the mixture before serving.
6. Serving Suggestion:
7. Garnish with chopped chives.

Nutritional Information Per Serving:
Calories: 619 Total Fat: 22.6 g Saturated Fat: 8.3 g Cholesterol: 217 mg Sodium: 1295 mg Total Carbohydrate: 36.1 g Dietary Fiber: 0.2 g Total Sugars: 35.2 g Protein: 66.6 g Potassium: 622 mg

Majestic Alfredo Chicken

Ingredients:

- 125 ml alfredo sauce
- 60 ml blue cheese, crumbled
- 4 slices provolone cheese
- 60 ml chicken seasoning
- 4 chicken breasts, halved
- 15 ml lemon juice
- 1 large apple wedged

Directions:

1. Take a medium-sized bowl and add chicken, alongside the seasoning.
2. Take another bowl and toss the apple with lemon.
3. Preheat your Ninja Foodi Grill in Med mode, set timer to 16 minutes.
4. Wait until you hear a beep sound.
5. Arrange chicken pieces to the grill grate and cook for about 8 minutes, flip and cook for 8 minutes.
6. Transfer the apple to the grill and cook for 4 minutes, giving 2 minutes to each side.
7. Serve grilled chicken with the blue cheese, apple, and alfredo sauce.
8. Enjoy!

Nutritional Values (Per Serving)
Calories: 247 Fat: 19 g Saturated Fat: 3 g Carbohydrates: 29 g Fiber: 2 g Sodium: 850 mg   Protein: 14 g

---

Excellent Chicken Tomatino

Ingredients:

- 2.5 ml salt
- 1 garlic clove, minced
- 30 ml olive oil
- 175 ml vinegar
- 8 plum tomatoes
- 60 ml fresh basil leaves
- 4 chicken breast, boneless and skinless

Directions:

1. Take your fine food processor and add olive oil, vinegar, salt, garlic, and basil. Blend the mixture well until you have a smooth texture.
2. Add tomatoes and blend once again.
3. Take a mixing bowl and add tomato mix, chicken and mix well.
4. Let the mixture chill for 1-2 hours.
5. Preheat your Ninja Foodi Grill to High and set the timer to 6 minutes.
6. Once you hear the beep, arrange your prepared chicken over the grill grate.
7. Cook for 3 minutes more.
8. Flip the chicken and cook for 3 minutes more.
9. Once properly cooked, serve and enjoy!

Nutritional Values (Per Serving)
Calories: 400 Fat: 5 g Saturated Fat: 3 g Carbohydrates: 18 g Fiber: 3 g Sodium: 230 mg Protein: 23 g

Chicken Parmesan

Ingredients:

- 2 chicken breasts, sliced into cutlets
- 90 ml seasoned bread crumbs
- 30 ml Parmesan cheese, grated
- 15 ml butter, melted
- 90 ml reduced-fat mozzarella cheese
- 125 ml marinara sauce
- Cooking spray

Directions:

1. Spray the Ninja Foodi basket with oil.
2. In a bowl, mix the bread crumbs and Parmesan cheese. In another bowl, place the butter. Coat the chicken with butter and dip into the bread crumb mix.
3. Place the cutlets on the basket. Seal the crisping lid. Set it to Air Crisp.
4. Cook at 190°C for 6 minutes.
5. Flip and top with the marinara and mozzarella.
6. Serving Suggestion:
7. Serve with pasta or salad.

Nutritional Information Per Serving:
Calories: 307 Total Fat: 14.4 g Saturated Fat: 6.5 g Cholesterol: 87 mg Sodium: 599 mg Total Carbohydrate: 13.3 g Dietary Fiber: 1.4 g Total Sugars: 3.4 g Protein: 30.8 g Potassium: 303 mg

Chicken Nuggets

Ingredients:

- 10 ml olive oil
- 90 ml breadcrumbs
- 30 ml grated parmesan cheese
- 2 chicken breasts, sliced into nuggets
- Salt and pepper to taste
- Cooking spray

Directions:

1. Pour the olive oil into one bowl.
2. In another bowl, mix the bread crumbs and Parmesan.
3. Season the chicken with salt and pepper.
4. Coat with the olive oil and dip in the bread crumb mixture.
5. Place the chicken on the basket. Seal the crisping lid. Select Air Crisp.
6. Cook at 190°C for 8 minutes.
7. Serving Suggestion:
8. Serve with a green salad or veggie sticks.

Nutritional Information Per Serving:
Calories: 245 Total Fat: 11.4 g Saturated Fat: 4 g Cholesterol: 75 mg Sodium: 267 mg Total Carbohydrate: 7.8 g Dietary Fiber: 0.5 g Total Sugars: 0.6 g
Protein: 27 g Potassium: 198 mg

Desserts

Simple fruit cake

Ingredients

- 425g mixed fruits or dried fruit
- 240g self-raising flour
- 500ml fruit juice *(see tips)*
- 2.5 ml baking powder

Method

1. Mix the mixed fruits or dried fruit *(see tips if using dried fruit)*, flour, baking powder, and fruit juice in a large mixing bowl.
2. Generously grease and flour a 7inch spring form pan.
3. Pour the batter into the greased pan and level the top with a spatula.
4. Add 350ml of water to the inner pot of your Ninja Foodi multi-cooker. Place the trivet or rack in its lowest position. Place the spring form pan on the rack.
5. Cover with the pressure-cooking lid and move the nozzle to seal. Select the PRESSURE function and cook on high for 1 hour.
6. Once the time is up, allow the multi-cooker to vent naturally for 10 minutes.

Tips

- You can also use iced coffee or tea in this recipe.
- If the dried fruit you are using has a sugar coating, rinse it in water.
- Soaking the fruits overnight will make them plump.
- If you wish to add nuts, do so as you combine the fruits with the flour.

Nutritional Information: *Calories – 145; Carbohydrates – 31.5g; Fat – 1g; Fibre – 1.5g; Protein – 3g; Sodium – 291mg; Sugar – 12g*

Egg custard

Ingredients

For the custard:

- 950ml whole milk or cream
- 6 large eggs
- 96g white Sugar
- 5 ml pure vanilla extract
- 1.25 ml ground cinnamon
- A pinch of sea salt

For garnish:

- Ground cinnamon
- Fresh fruit or berries
- Freshly grated nutmeg

Method

1. Mix the milk, vanilla, sugar, and salt in a medium-sized bowl. Blend until combined thoroughly, but do not ov mix.
2. Divide the mixture into 6 oven-safe ramekins or custard cups. Cover them with aluminium foil and make sm venting holes with a skewer.
3. Add 350ml water to the inner pot of the multi-cooker. Place the trivet or rack in the pot and then place the ramek or custard cups on top of the rack (you may need to cook in batches).
4. Put the pressure-cooking lid on and seal it. Select PRESSURE mode and cook for 2 minutes on high.
5. Once the timer beeps, allow the multi-cooker to vent the pressure naturally for 10 minutes. If there is a small amo of whey on top of the custard, discard it. Set aside the cooked egg custards and cook the remaining custards.
6. Serve with your preferred garnish.

***Nutritional Information** (garnish not included):* Calories – 324; Carbohydrates – 46.5g; Fat – 10g; Fibre – 0.1g; Protein – 12g; Sodium 203mg; Sugar – 46g

Peach upside-down cake

Ingredients

- 3 peaches, skin removed and sliced
- 180g plain flour
- 150g light brown sugar (plus 100g), divided
- 75g butter (plus 4 tbsp.), divided
- 10g baking powder
- 160ml milk
- 1 egg
- 5 ml ground cinnamon
- 1.25 ml nutmeg
- A pinch of salt

Method

1. Grease a 7inch pan with butter and set it aside.
2. Set the multi-cooker to SEAR/SAUTÉ mode, and then melt 60 ml butter and 100g sugar in the inner pot. Once melted, add this caramel to the greased pan and arrange the peach slices in it.
3. Beat the remaining 150g sugar and 75g butter in a stand mixer. Add the egg and milk, and then beat again until fully incorporated.
4. Fold in the flour, nutmeg, cinnamon, baking powder and salt.
5. Pour the batter into the pan and cover the pan with aluminium foil.
6. Set the trivet or rack in the lowest position inside the multi-cooker pot.
7. Place the pan on the trivet or rack. Put the pressure lid on and secure the nozzle to seal. Select the PRESSURE function and cook on high for 20 minutes.
8. Once the time is up, let the multi-cooker release the pressure naturally for 10 minutes. Use the quick release to vent out the remaining pressure.
9. Use oven gloves to take the pan out.
10. Remove the foil and let the cake cool for a few minutes.
11. Run a knife around the edges of the cake and turn it out onto a plate.
12. Serve warm with a scoop of ice cream.

Nutritional Information (without the ice cream): Calories – 355; Carbohydrates – 51g; Fat – 15g; Fibre – 1g; Protein – 4g; Sodium – 103mg; Sugar – 32.7g

Chocolate pot de crème

Ingredients

- 170g chocolate
- 128g double cream
- 32g sugar
- 125 ml full-fat milk
- 5 ml espresso powder
- 3 egg yolks
- 5 ml vanilla extract
- A pinch of salt

For toppings:

- Whipping cream
- Sprinkles

Method

1. Pour the milk and double cream into the inner pot of the Ninja Foodi multi-cooker. Select the SEAR/SAUTÉ function and set it to high. Turn the multi-cooker off as soon as the mixture begins to bubble.
2. Mix the chocolate chips and espresso powder in a mixing bowl. Pour in the milk-cream mixture to melt the chocolate chips.
3. Crack the eggs and place the yolks in a separate mixing bowl (discard the egg whites). Add the sugar and whisk 5 minutes or until the yolk colour has lightened. Add salt and vanilla and whisk again to combine.
4. Stir the chocolate a few times. Once fully melted, pour the in-egg mixture in a steady stream whilst whisking constantly. Whisk for 4 to 5 minutes or until the chocolate starts to thicken slightly.
5. Spoon the chocolate mixture into the jars, making sure to leave at least a quarter of an inch of space at the top. Screw the jar lids on and put them inside the air fryer basket.
6. Meanwhile, pour 235ml of water into the inner pot of the multi-cooker. Set the air fryer basket inside the pot, put the pressure lid, and set the nozzle to seal. Select PRESSURE mode and cook on low for 5 minutes.
7. Once the timer beeps, let the multi-cooker vent naturally for 5 minutes before using the quick release.
8. Let the jars cool for a bit, then chill them in the fridge for at least 4 hours.
9. Top with whipped cream and sprinkles before serving.

Tip

- You will need 6 120ml pressure-safe canning jars.

Nutritional Information (without the toppings): Calories – 371; Carbohydrates – 28g; Fat – 27g; Fibre – 2g; Protein – 4g; Sodium – 33mg; Sugar – 24g

Victoria sponge cake

Ingredients

For the sponge cake:

- 450g caster sugar
- 400g self-raising flour
- 200g butter, softened
- 50g lemon curd
- 480ml skimmed milk
- 4 medium eggs
- 60 ml strawberry jam
- 15 ml vanilla essence
- 15 ml extra-virgin olive oil

For the butter cream:

- 210g icing sugar
- 115g butter
- 15 ml single cream
- 5 ml vanilla essence
- 5 ml maple syrup
- 2.5 ml strawberry food colouring

Method

1. Using a hand mixer, beat the butter and sugar in a bowl.
2. Add the eggs, olive oil, and vanilla essence, and then mix again.
3. When the mixture is creamy, add the lemon curd, milk and flour. Mix with a wooden spoon to avoid over-mixing. You need a creamy but thin batter; if you find it is too thick, add a bit more milk or water –1tbsp. at a time will do.
4. Spritz non-stick spray on your cake pans, and then dust them with flour to make floured surfaces.
5. Divide the batter evenly between the two pans. Tap each pan on the counter (or table) a few times to release bubbles and even out the top of your cake.
6. Place one cake pan inside the Ninja Foodi and close the crisping lid.
7. Select AIR FRY mode and cook for 10 minutes at 180°C. Once the timer beeps, switch the temperature to 160 and cook for further 16 minutes.
8. Carefully remove the first cake pan from the cooker. Insert the second one and repeat the previous step. Let first cake cool down completely.
9. Meanwhile, beat the butter and icing sugar in a bowl. Add the remaining butter cream ingredients and continue to mix until you achieve a creamy consistency. Chill in the fridge as you wait for the cakes to cool.

10. Once the cakes are completely cooled, remove the filling from the fridge. Slice the cake tops off so that it will be easier to stick them together.
11. Add a layer of strawberry jam, then a layer of butter cream before bringing the two cakes together.
12. Refrigerate the cake for at least an hour before serving. *(see tips)*

ps

- ~ You will need 2 cake pans that fit inside your Ninja Foodi.
- ~ Skimmed milk helps the cake to stay moist, which is crucial to this recipe.
- ~ Step 12 is crucial as it will help you slice the cake.

Nutritional Information: *Calories – 613; Carbohydrates – 89g; Fat – 25g; Fibre – g; Protein – 8g; Sodium – 242mg; Sugar – 63g*

Sticky toffee pudding

Ingredients

For the cake:

- 150g plain flour
- 130g dates, pitted and diced
- 55g unsalted butter (plus more for greasing), softened and divided
- 55g brown sugar
- 60ml water
- 60ml milk
- 1 egg
- 5 ml baking powder
- 1.25 ml baking soda

For the caramel sauce:

- 180ml 35% cream
- 160g brown sugar

Method

1. Grease a 6inch spring form pan with butter.
2. In a small pot, bring the 60ml water and dates to a boil before stirring in the baking soda. Turn off the heat a let it cool.
3. Mix the flour and baking powder in a bowl.
4. In another bowl, beat the butter and sugar with an electric mixer. Add the egg and continue to beat until smoo Set the electric mixer to a low speed and add the dry mixture, alternating with the date mixture and milk. O everything is combined well, pour the batter into the greased pan.
5. Place a trivet or rack inside the multi-cooker's inner pot and add 375ml water. Place the spring form pan on of the trivet or rack.
6. Put the pressure-cooking lid on and secure the nozzle to seal. Select PRESSURE mode and cook on high for minutes.
7. Once done, let the multi-cooker vent the pressure naturally for 10 minutes. Use the quick release to vent out remaining pressure.
8. Take out the spring form pan with oven gloves and set it aside.
9. Take out the rack and discard the remaining water. Wipe the inner pot dry.
10. To make the caramel sauce, place the cream and brown sugar in the inner pot.
11. Select SEAR/SAUTÉ mode and cook on high until the cream and sugar start to boil. Let it simmer for 2 minu then press the START/STOP button to stop.
12. Pour the caramel sauce over the cake and serve.

- Perform a toothpick test to determine whether the cake is thoroughly cooked. Insert a toothpick in the middle of the cake and if it comes out clean, then the cake is cooked.

Nutritional Information: Calories – 470; Carbohydrates – 72g; Fat – 18g; Fibre – 2.4g; Protein – 5g; Sodium – 91mg; Sugar – 50g

Gingerbread pudding cake

Preparation: 10 minutes | Cooking: 50 minutes | Yields: 5

Ingredients

For the batter:

- 170g plain flour
- 96g sugar
- 65g treacle or molasses
- 32g butter, softened
- 120ml water
- 1 egg
- 5 ml ground ginger
- 3.75 ml baking soda
- 2.5 ml cinnamon
- 1.25 ml nutmeg
- 1.25 ml clove powder
- 1.25 ml allspice
- 1.25 ml salt

For sprinkling over batter:

- 32g light brown sugar

For the sauce:

- 235ml hot water
- 60 ml butter, melted

Method

1. Grease a 7inch round pan with the softened butter then set aside.
2. Whisk the flour, spices, baking soda, and salt in a medium-sized bowl.
3. Beat the butter and sugar in a stand mixer until combined.
4. Add the egg and beat again to combine.
5. Add the treacle or molasses and beat at medium speed.
6. Add the water and beat again to combine. The mixture should appear to have curdled at this point.
7. Switch the stand-in mixer to a slower speed, and then add the flour mixture in 3parts. Beat gently to incorpor it well.
8. Pour the batter into the greased round pan. Sprinkle the top with brown sugar in an even layer.
9. Mix the hot water and melted butter in a bowl, then pour the mixture over the brown sugar topping.
10. Place a trivet or rack in the inner pot of the Ninja Foodi multi-cooker. Pour 355ml of water into the pot.

11. Place the round pan on the rack or trivet. Cover the pot with the pressure-cooking lid and secure the nozzle to seal.
12. Choose PRESSURE mode and cook on high for 50 minutes.
13. Once done, let the multi-cooker vent the pressure naturally.
14. Open the lid, take out the pan and let the cake sit for 5 minutes.
15. Serve warm with a scoop of ice cream.

Nutritional Information (without the ice cream): *Calories – 531; Carbohydrates – 86g; Fat – 19g; Fibre – 1g; Protein – 4g; Sodium – 475mg; Sugar – 66g*

Appendix 1: Measurement Conversion Table Volume Equivalents (Liquid)

US Standard	US Standard (Ounces)	Metric (Approximate)
2 tablespoons	1 fl. oz.	30 mL
¼ cup	2 fl. oz.	60 mL
½ cup	4 fl. oz.	120 mL
1 cup	8 fl. oz.	240 mL
1 and ½ cups	12 fl. oz.	355 mL
2 cups/1 pint	16 fl. oz.	475 mL
4 cups/ 1 quart	32 fl. oz.	1 L
1 gallon	128 fl. oz.	4 L

Volume Equivalents (Dry)

US Standard	Metric (Approximate)
1/8 teaspoon	0.5 mL
¼ teaspoon	1 mL
½ teaspoon	2 mL
¾ teaspoon	4 mL
1 teaspoon	5 mL

1 tablespoon	15 mL
¼ cup	58 mL
1/3 cup	79 mL
½ cup	117 mL
2/3 cup	156 mL
¾ cup	177 mL
1 cup	235 mL
2 cups	475 mL
3 cups	700 mL
4 cups	1 L

Oven Temperatures

Fahrenheit (F)	Celsius (C) (Approximate)
250°	120°
300°	150°
325°	165°
350°	180°
375°	190°

400	200
425	220
450	230

Weight Equivalents

US Standard	Metric (Approximate)
½ ounce	15 g
1 ounce	30 g
2 ounces	60 g
4 ounces	115 g
8 ounces	225 g
12 ounces	340 g
16 ounces/1 pound	455 g

Appendix II: Healthy Food List For Weight Loss And Keto

Nowadays, too many people want to lose weight and get healthy! Keto Diet has many followers in this world. If you are one of t followers, while you are on a Keto Diet, you should consider keeping the following ingredients in your plate in order to g maximum benefits from your diet!

- Various types of nuts and seeds such as Brazil Nuts, Almonds, Cashews, Pecans, Macadamia, Pistachio, Walnu Chia Seeds, Flaxseeds etc.
- Various types of healthy cheese that are rich in calcium, protein and essential fatty acids
- Avocados
- Fresh meat and chicken/poultry. Try to opt for Grass-Fed meat as Unsweetened Tea and Coffee (in controll amounts)
- Seafood such as Salmon, Mussels, Clams, Oysters, Mackerel, Sardines etc.
- Dark Chocolate and Cocoa Powder
- much as possible
- Eggs
- Coconut Oil
- Cottage Cheese/ Plain Greek Yogurt
- Low carb veggies such as Brussels, spinach, broccoli, cauliflower, zucchini etc.
- Olive Oil
- Various kinds of berries such as Strawberries, Blueberries, Blackberries, Raspberries
- Cream and Butter

- Shirataki Noodles
- Olives

...ose are the ingredients that you should try to keep around as much as possible. Asides from that, below is a full list of the all ...d that allowed or restricted while on a Keto Diet. **Meats and Animal Produce:** While choosing your meat, always make sure ...avoid farmed animal meats and processed meats such as sausages or hot dogs.

...y to go for the animal meats and animal-derived products:

- Grass-fed meat such as lamb, venison, beef, lamb, chicken, rabbit, etc.
- Offal from grass-fed animals: kidney, liver, tripe, tongue, etc
- Ghee
- Seafood caught in the wild such as caviar, crab, mussels, clams, and scallops
- Pastured eggs
- Butter
- Gelatin
- Pastured poultry and pork
- Wild caught fish such as cod, mackerel, tuna, eel, etc.

ts: Try to take more saturated and Monosaturated varieties of fat.

- 90% or higher dark chocolate
- Saturated fats include lard, tallow, duck fat, chicken fat, ghee, etc.
- Palm shortening
- Chia seeds
- Fats rich in poly-saturated Omega-3s extracted from animal sources
- Monounsaturated fats include avocado oil, olive oil, and macadamia oil
- Cocoa butter, coconut butter

Vegetables: When choosing your vegetable, try to avoid root vegetables and stick to the green leafy ones as they will help you keep your carbohydrates level at a minimum.

- Watercress
- Zucchini
- Shallots
- Seaweeds
- Fennel
- Cucumber
- Spinach
- Tomatoes
- Chives
- Cauliflower
- Pumpkin
- Scallions
- Radishes
- Okra
- Onions
- Mushrooms
- All leafy greens
- Lettuce
- Garlic
- Bell Pepper
- Asparagus
- Artichokes

- Chives
- Celery
- Carrots
- Cabbage
- Broccoli

Fruits: Regarding a Ketogenic diet, most fruits are off the table, mainly because of the high level of fructose. However, small amounts of berries are allowed.

Good choices for fruits are:

- Blackberry
- Lime
- Strawberry
- Cranberry
- Lemon
- Avocado
- Olives
- Blueberry
- Raspberry

Legumes: Similar to fruits, all types of legumes are off the table. However, a very small amount of peas or green beans can be included in your diet.

Dairy Products: In general, the following dairy products are good for your soul

- Full fat raw cheese
- Full fat cottage cheese
- Kefir
- Ghee

- ❖ Butter
- ❖ Full fat yogurt
- ❖ Heavy whipping cream
- ❖ Full fat sour cream
- ❖ Full fat cream cheese

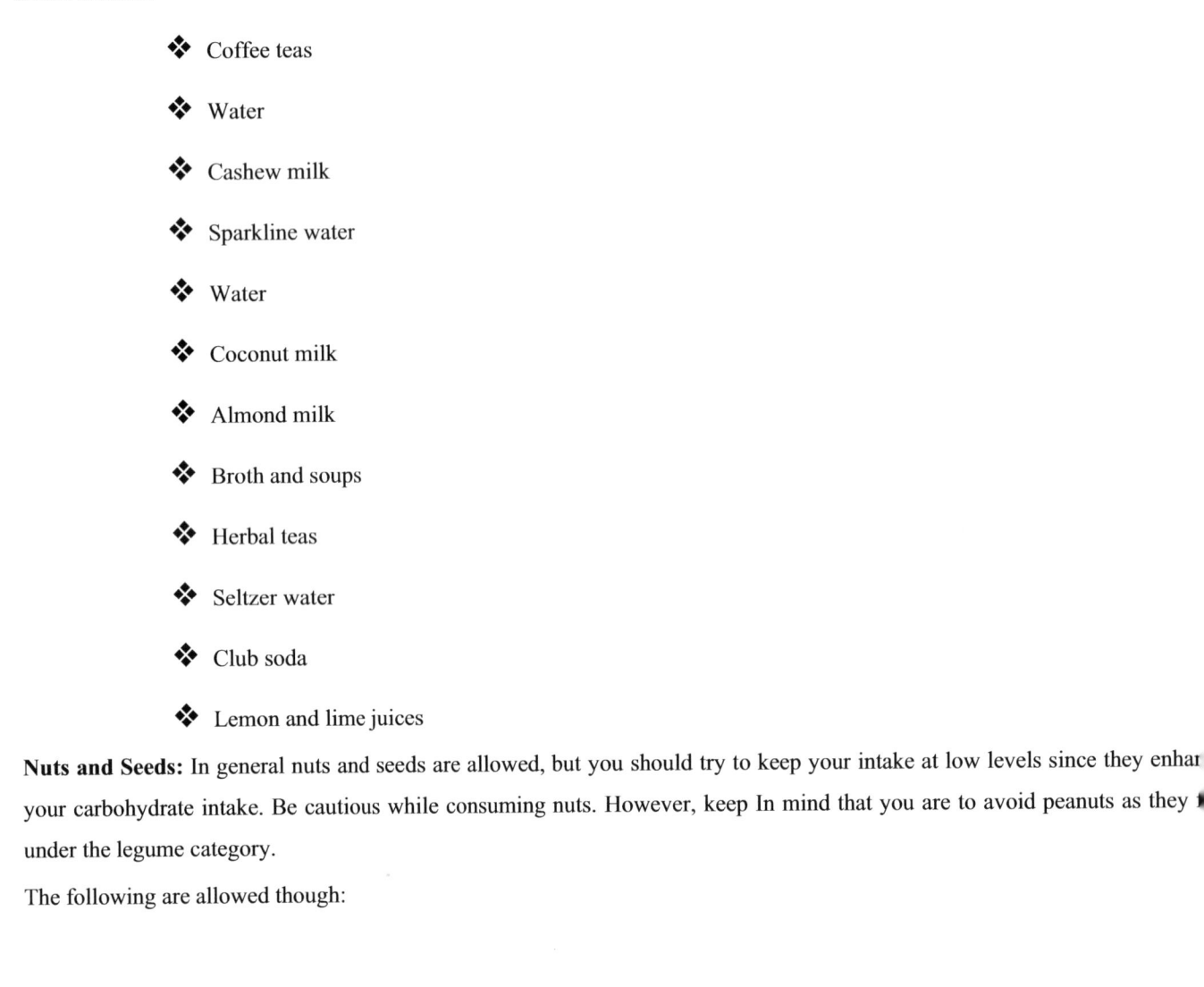

Drinks: All types of sweet or aerated drinks are to be avoided entirely in your Keto diet. Drink of plenty of water though! Good drinks include:

- ❖ Coffee teas
- ❖ Water
- ❖ Cashew milk
- ❖ Sparkline water
- ❖ Water
- ❖ Coconut milk
- ❖ Almond milk
- ❖ Broth and soups
- ❖ Herbal teas
- ❖ Seltzer water
- ❖ Club soda
- ❖ Lemon and lime juices

Nuts and Seeds: In general nuts and seeds are allowed, but you should try to keep your intake at low levels since they enhance your carbohydrate intake. Be cautious while consuming nuts. However, keep In mind that you are to avoid peanuts as they fall under the legume category.

The following are allowed though:

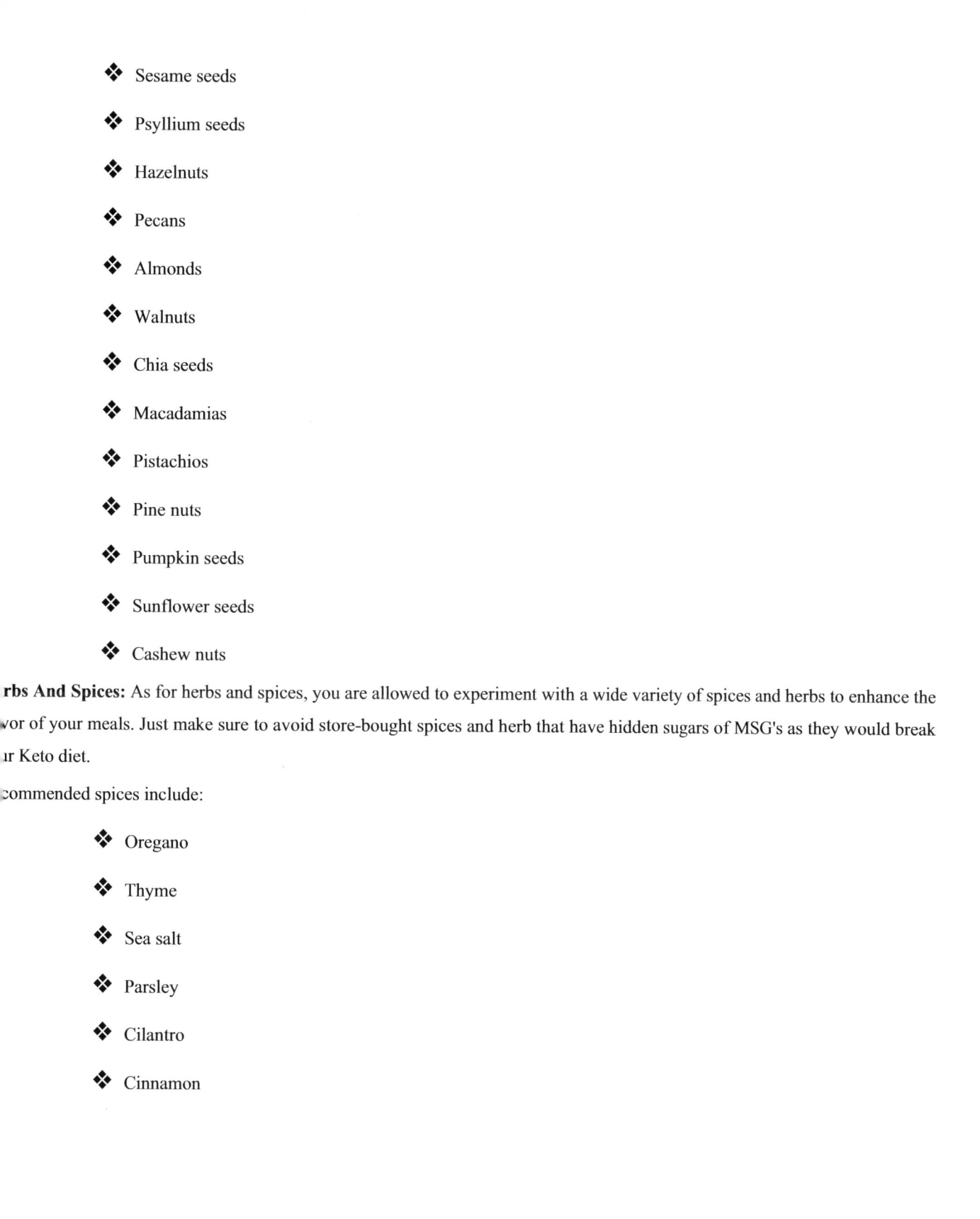

- ❖ Sesame seeds
- ❖ Psyllium seeds
- ❖ Hazelnuts
- ❖ Pecans
- ❖ Almonds
- ❖ Walnuts
- ❖ Chia seeds
- ❖ Macadamias
- ❖ Pistachios
- ❖ Pine nuts
- ❖ Pumpkin seeds
- ❖ Sunflower seeds
- ❖ Cashew nuts

Herbs And Spices: As for herbs and spices, you are allowed to experiment with a wide variety of spices and herbs to enhance the flavor of your meals. Just make sure to avoid store-bought spices and herb that have hidden sugars of MSG's as they would break your Keto diet.

Recommended spices include:

- ❖ Oregano
- ❖ Thyme
- ❖ Sea salt
- ❖ Parsley
- ❖ Cilantro
- ❖ Cinnamon

- Basil
- Chili powder
- Black pepper
- White pepper
- Curry powder
- Italian seasoning
- Cumin powder
- Sage
- Ginger
- Cardamom
- Rosemary
- Turmeric
- Cloves
- Allspices
- Paprika

-Day Meal Plan to Enjoy Your Foodi Day By Day

Week 1

Week 1	Saturday	Sunday	Monday	Tuesday	Wednesday	Thursday	Friday
Breakfast	Cheesed Up Air Sticks	Classic Dutch Pancakes	Excellent Mushroom And Garlic Flavored Packs	Cinnamon And Pineapple Grill	Perfect Breakfast Sausage	Crispy Caramelized Morning Pop Corns	Classy Pickle Fries
Lunch	Gentle And Simple Stew	Broccoli Fish casserole	Vegetable tart	Grilled Chicken with Veggies	Sweet sriracha carrots	Hearty Swordfish Meal	Black beans in tomato sauce
Dinner	Grilled Chicken with Veggies	Cool Shrimp Zoodles	Sweet sriracha carrots	Buttered Up Scallops	Vegetable tart	Chicken Nuggets	Broccoli casserole
Dessert	Simple fruit cake	Egg custard	Chocolate pot de crème	Victoria sponge cake	Gingerbread pudding cake	Sticky toffee pudding	Peach upside-down cake

Week 2

	Saturday	Sunday	Monday	Tuesday	Wednesday	Thursday	Friday
Breakfast	Excellent Mushroom And Garlic Flavored Packs	Cinnamon And Pineapple Grill	Cheesed Up Air Sticks	Perfect Breakfast Sausage	Classic Dutch Pancakes	Awesome French Toasted Sticks	Crispy Caramelized Morning Pop Corns
Lunch	Hearty Swordfish Meal	Peanut Chicken	Broccoli casserole	Vegetable tart	Gentle And Simple Fish Stew	Sweet sriracha carrots	Chicken Parmesan
Dinner	Buttered Up Scallops	Sweet sriracha carrots	Vegetable tart	Black beans in tomato sauce	Peanut Chicken	Cool Shrimp Zoodles	Broccoli casserole
Dessert	Chocolate pot de crème	Simple fruit cake	Victoria sponge cake	Egg custard	Peach upside-down cake	Gingerbread pudding cake	Sticky toffee pudding

Week 3

Week 3	Saturday	Sunday	Monday	Tuesday	Wednesday	Thursday	Friday
Breakfast	Crispy Caramelized Morning Pop Corns	Classic Dutch Pancakes	Excellent Mushroom And Garlic Flavored Packs	Awesome Crispy Egg Rolls	Perfect Breakfast Sausage	Cheesed Up Air Sticks	Cinnamon And Pineapple Grill
Lunch	Small-Time Herby Cods	Honey Chicken Wings	Vegetable tart	Sweet sriracha carrots	Awesome Sock-Eye Salmon	Broccoli casserole	Excellent Chicken Tomatino
Dinner	Broccoli casserole	Awesome Cherry Tomato Mackerel	Sweet sriracha carrots	Cauliflower puree with scallions	Honey Chicken Wings	Heartfelt Sesame Fish	Vegetable tart
Dessert	Peach upside-down cake	Victoria sponge cake	Egg custard	Sticky toffee pudding	Simple fruit cake	Gingerbread pudding cake	Chocolate pot de crème

Week 4

Week 4	Saturday	Sunday	Monday	Tuesday	Wednesday	Thursday	Friday
Breakfast	Perfect Breakfast Sausage	Early Morning Pumpkin Muffins	Crispy Caramelized Morning Pop Corns	Excellent Mushroom And Garlic Flavored Packs	Cinnamon And Pineapple Grill	Classic Dutch Pancakes	Cheesed Up Air Sticks
Lunch	Small-Time Herby Cods	Vegetable tart	Honey & Rosemary Chicken	Sweet sriracha carrots	Broccoli casserole	Awesome Sock-Eye Salmon	Roasted veggie mix
Dinner	Heartfelt Sesame Fish	Sweet sriracha carrots	Broccoli casserole	Awesome Cherry Tomato Mackerel	Majestic Alfredo Chicken	Vegetable tart	Honey & Rosemary Chicken
Dessert	Chocolate pot de crème	Egg custard	Sticky toffee pudding	Peach upside-down cake	Gingerbread pudding cake	Victoria sponge cake	Simple fruit cake

Conclusion

I can't express how honored I am to think that you found my book interesting and informative enough to read it all through to the end.

I thank you again for purchasing this book and I hope that you had as much fun reading it as I had writing it.

I bid you farewell and encourage you to move forward with your amazing Ninja Foodi

Printed in Great Britain
by Amazon